Daily Mirror

KEN

3d. Saturday, November 23, 1963 No. 18,640

ASSASSINATED

Seconds after the shot . . . Mrs. Kennedy bends over her dying husband. Standing on the car bumper is a Secret Service man.

Jackie holds dying husband

THE world was horror-struck last night by the news that America's President John F. Kennedy was dead—shot down by a hidden assassin.

Mr. Kennedy, only forty-six and the leader of the West, was riding in an open car with his wife Jackie in Dallas, Texas.

A bullet ripped through his head. He fell forward, and his 34-year-old wife cradled his head in her arms.

As the car raced to a nearby hospital, Jackie kept crying: "Oh, no!" Her clothes were spattered with blood.

Mr. Kennedy lived only twenty-five minutes after he was hit. In hospital, surgeons opened his throat to relieve breathing and to give him blood.

But he died—at about 1 p.m., local time, 7 p.m. British time. And shocked millions throughout the world heard the announcement soon afterwards.

Texan Governor John Connally, 46, who was in the Presidential car, was also hit by one of the assassin's three shots. After an operation his condition was satisfactory.

Waiting

Last night, police were questioning a Texan who had once defected to Russia. They had found a rifle with a telescopic sight. And they said that the assassin had been eating fried chicken at a sixth-floor window while waiting for the President.

Mr. Kennedy was the fourth United States President to be assassinated.

Automatically, Vice-President Lyndon B. Johnson, 55, takes over at the White House.

Last night, as he was sworn in as President in the plane taking Mr. Kennedy's body to Washington, world leaders spoke with deep emotion of the youngest man ever to be President of the United States.

Full dramatic story by RALPH CHAMPION, Chief of the Mirror's American Bureau— *see Back Page*

WHEN I WAS YOUNG
THE SIXTIES

LO[illegible] [illegible]TO

Susan Forbes was born in 1952 in Cheltenham, in Gloucestershire. She lived with her parents and her two sisters in Gretton, a small village near Cheltenham. She went first to the village school, and then to grammar school in Cheltenham. On leaving school, she trained to become a nurse and worked in local hospitals after qualifying.

Susan married while she was training to be a nurse and has three children. She has since remarried and still lives in the Cheltenham area.

Susan now runs a consultancy firm which she set up with a friend in Cheltenham. She advises charities on fund-raising, and organises charity events.

First published in Great Britain by
Franklin Watts Limited
96 Leonard Street
London EC2A 4RH

Franklin Watts Australia
14 Mars Road
Lane Cove
N.S.W. 2066

ISBN: 0 7496 0237 6

CONTENTS

Me and my family

I was born in 1952 in Cheltenham in Gloucestershire. I was christened Susan Jane Bliss, and was the first of three sisters. We lived with our parents in a small house in a village called Gretton, about sixteen kilometres from Cheltenham.

When I was little, my dad worked as a sales rep for a local firm selling wallpaper and paint. Mum looked after the three of us girls. Later on, when we were all much older, she got a job as the school secretary in the village.

When I was about eleven, Dad started working for himself. He did posh decorating. He bought a van, and painted his name on a board which he screwed to the side. He used to do quite grand houses, and he even painted a few of the nearby churches in the Cotswolds.

Our house has been extended a lot since we first lived there.

Mum, Dad and us girls at a party.

Me and my sisters, Helen and Debbie.

My grandma and grandpa.

My grandparents lived in Cheltenham in a council house. Sometimes I'd stay with them by myself. That always felt very grown-up. Everything was painted mushroom colour and there was no heating, so it was ever so cold. Grandpa would sit down while my grandma read him the newspaper. He could read perfectly well but Grandma was just bossy. I'd listen too, and that way I got to know quite a bit of what was happening in the news.

There were two pubs and one shop in the village. The New Inn by the school had a hatch in the side where you could knock and get four sweets for a penny. We called it the P.U.B. because it wasn't nice to say "pub".

The same pub now.

The New Inn in the 1960s.

My sisters and I used to go out with Dad on his rounds all across the Cotswolds. He had a smart, new, black Hillman Minx with a two-way radio to keep in touch with his office. The radio took up half the back seat. When he went into a shop to try and make a sale, he told us to stay in the car. But within three minutes we'd be hooting the horn and trying to call his office on the radio handset. His call sign was "Clara".

I was a bit bossy with my sisters and did once get really horrible with the little one. When she was six I told her the family didn't want her any more. I took her to the Post Office over the road and said I had to send her away. The children in the village always said the woman who ran the Post Office then was a witch, so Debbie must have been really scared.

My sisters and I in Dad's car.

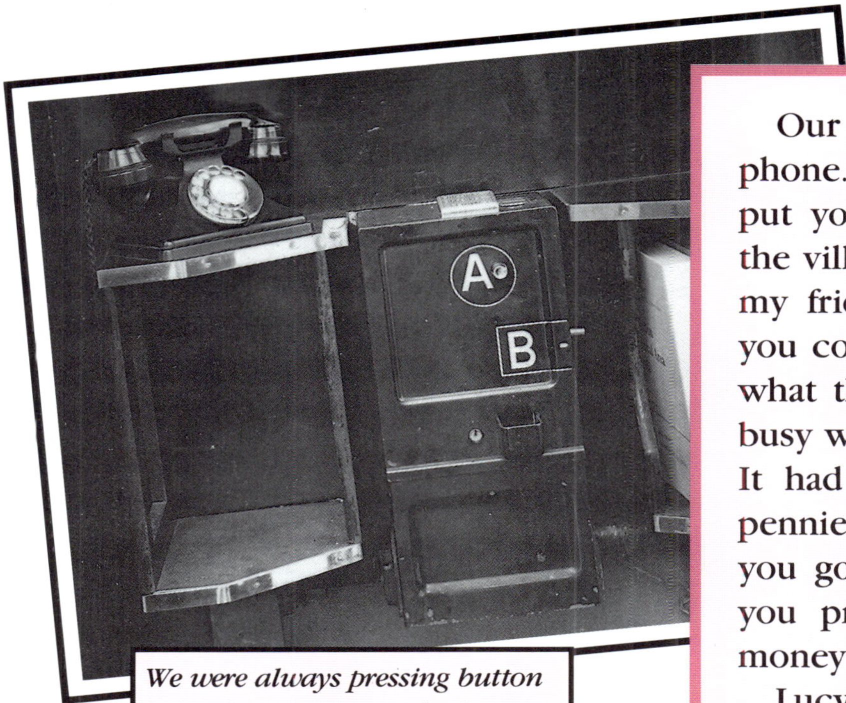

We were always pressing button B just in case anyone had forgotten their money.

Our house had an old black telephone. You had to call the operator to put you through to anywhere outside the village. We shared a party line with my friend Lucy's house, which meant you could pick up the phone and hear what they were saying. If the line was busy we had to use the public call box. It had two buttons. You put in four pennies and pressed button A when you got through. If nobody answered, you pressed button B and got your money back.

Lucy's parents were divorced – that hardly ever happened in our village then. Her mum was a potter and she was so busy she never noticed the kids hadn't gone to bed. I thought Lucy's freedom was wonderful; in our house we had rules. I'd get into terrible trouble for not being home for bedtime, even if I'd just been chatting or reading with my friends and lost track of the time.

Lucy and I read a lot of comics. Judy *and* Girl *were my favourites. It was a real treat to get a comic annual for Christmas.*

School

I'd been at the little village school down the road since I was four. There were just two teachers, one for the four- to seven-year-olds and one for the seven to elevens. There were only five other kids my age. We all sat the "eleven plus" exam, even the ones who couldn't read and write. I was the only one who passed, and that meant I got a place at the "girls only" grammar school in Cheltenham.

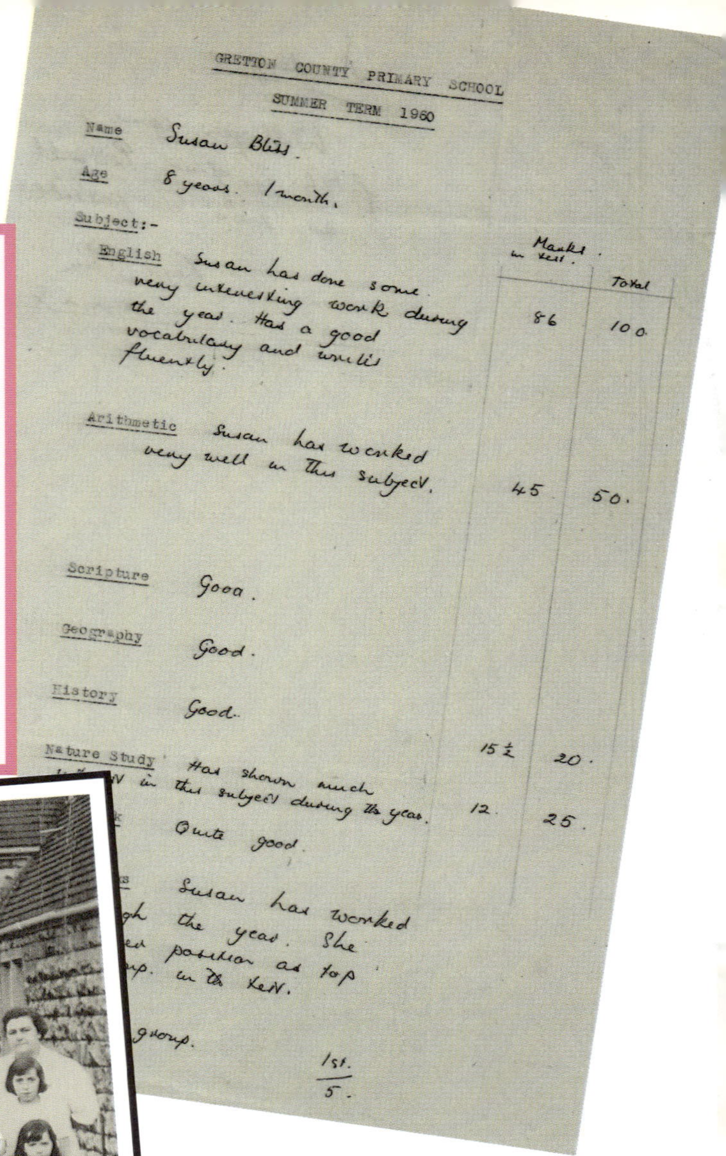
GRETTON COUNTY PRIMARY SCHOOL
SUMMER TERM 1960

Name: Susan Bliss.
Age: 8 years. 1 month.
Subject:-

Subject	Remarks	Marks in test	Total
English	Susan has done some very interesting work during the year. Has a good vocabulary and writes fluently.	86	100.
Arithmetic	Susan has worked very well in this subject.	45	50.
Scripture	Good.		
Geography	Good.		
History	Good.		
Nature Study	Has shown much ... in this subject during the year.	15½	20.
		12.	25.
	Quite good.		

Susan has worked ... the year. She ... position as top ... in the test.

... group.

1st.
5.

Gretton Primary School in 1956.
Susan is in the front row.

Gretton School now has twice as many children as it had in Susan's day.

There were a hundred and twenty girls in each year and all of them seemed cleverer than me.

Going to the grammar school was a bit of a shock. It was all fearfully polite and old-fashioned. We had to walk on the left-hand side of the corridor and we weren't allowed to run indoors. There was a misconduct book, and you'd get a mark if you did something like letting a door go on a teacher, or if you were seen without your hat in the street. If you got three marks in one term you'd be sent home with a note saying you couldn't come back till you'd learnt to behave.

There was a very strict uniform. We had a grey skirt, red jumper and a hat which had to be worn outside at all times. If anyone was spotted in Cheltenham wearing the school sweater and doing something they shouldn't, then the whole school heard about it. It didn't have to be anything really serious either; one girl was expelled just for wearing eye make-up while she was in uniform.

Me aged fifteen, doing my homework.

Some of the Upper Sixth in 1963.

Lots of things were forbidden by the headmistress. She completely terrified us. She used to go around with a ruler, checking the length of our skirts. Most of us had them rolled over at the waist to make them shorter, but we'd let them down to be measured then roll them back up again. There had to be three inches between the top of our socks and the hem of our skirts. Even when mini-skirts came in, there was still the ruler.

The new art college was built on the edge of the school grounds. We were told not to talk to the art students. The school even cordoned off the field so we couldn't go near. It seemed terribly exciting beyond the hedge. Some girls did get across to see the students, I think they were a bit disappointed after all the fuss.

… had missed the first half of the … was fervently wishing I had stayed at home and watched television. Mercifully the curtains closed for the interval and I was able to leap out of my velvet trap, fall over six pairs of feet and a hand-bag and make an ungracious exit in the general direction of the cloak-room. Here I spent the pleasantest quarter of an hour, sitting quietly on a squeaky chair with a damp towel pressed to my forehead. Then it was time to stroll casually back into that perfumed arbour of accidents, sink into the velvet seat and enjoy the second half of the play.

On my way in, I had noticed a polite sign requesting the audience not to smoke. For a few moments I wondered if I was seated in front of a lady or a steam engine. I choked, spluttered, cringed before the angry glares of my delightful neighbours and quietly resolved never to touch another cigarette.

There is little more to tell. I sat through two more hectic scenes and finally decided that the discontented murmurs were meant, not for the actors, but for me. I took the only course left to me. I left. . . .

Your half hour is now over and if you so wish, you may phone for a car. However, you may have come to the conclusion that it would be wise to take the advice of one who has learned f… inful experience. Believe me … your own snug … d on the square

I had a story in the school magazine.

…ELOPE POWELL (V.S)

MY WAY HOME

I am coming home from school on a warm spring day. The time is about five o'clock, only a few birds are twittering and the sun is slowly sinking. As I get off the bus, everywhere there is peace. I pass our small village shop which is closed, as it is Thursday, but I see Mrs. Coles has been busy putting up a fence on the edge of her garden to keep off the dogs. Now I see the church to my left and one or two council houses on the right. In the churchyard I notice a new grave so I know there has been a funeral earlier today. As I go on up the road, I see a large thrush which flies away at the noise of my footsteps. I pass under the old railway bridge, which is now used only a few times a day, and on the banks of the line I see thousands of primroses. Now to my right is the old vicarage and to my left are only fields ; and now I see a farm where a few cows are waiting to be milked.

Near the Infants' School all is quiet and deserted, but I can see that the grass and shrubs which were planted in the Autumn are now coming along splendidly. Almost opposite the school is a place which

26

is supposed to be haunted. Next I see our disused chapel, looking rather forlorn, but to brighten the scene are one or two small birds having a mud bath. Soon another farm and the Coronation seat come into view. In the background, behind the latter are three smallish half-timbered cottages and amongst these stands the old Saxon Tower.

My friend Beryl, is on her pony, Trigger, under a large horse-chestnut tree. I stop for a few moments and talk to her, but I am in need of some tea, so I hurry on. There stands the old forge with rose trees and cabbages in the garden, and although Mrs. Borstock has put tin foil on sticks to frighten the birds away, a large jackdaw is sitting on a rose tree. Now I cross the road, pass the telephone booth and see my own drive with the large horsechestnut tree at the bottom and the sign, "T. J. Bliss, Builder" hanging on the wall by the gate post. We have tall wooden gates with large gate posts. I go through the gates and see my guinea pig, Sandy, running about loose on the lawn ; I also spot my cat, Smokey, sitting in the sun, so I drop all my things, chase Sandy into her cage, shut the door and go up the drive, noticing, as I pass, some new plants Mummy has put in during the day. I enter our loggia door and smell an appetizing curry cooking so I rush in to reach it more quickly.

SUSAN BLISS (I.S)

TABULA RASA

Cold in a window of sunlight
She sits and regrets her sitting,
While mounds of mending and knitting
Attend her erratic pleasure.
She wonders why her being
Has chosen this street to measure
Itself against. Being so fleeting,
Could it not have found jewelled danger ?
In her wondering, is there anger ?
What will supply the answer ?
Not the phalanx of books on the shelf,
Nor the shivering plates on the dresser,
Nor the slumbering rug at the hearth :
These are permanent things that depress her.
But her child who plays in the garden,
And her father, long dead in his picture:
These are the ropes of blood
That tie her to past and future.
Would reading their temporary, dull eyes
Reveal the damning answer ?
The answer ! But John is coming home
And supper not made. It's not clever
To drown in dreams. The answer ?
But the question is gone for ever.

SUSAN LIMB (U.VI)

SHORT CUTS TO THE COUNTRYSIDE

In many poets inspiration is aroused by one particular aspect of life, because of their fascination with this subject. Thus we connect Owen with war, Brooke with England and patriotism, and Masefield with the sea. Hardy, Frost, Betjeman and Thomas are four modern poets who

27

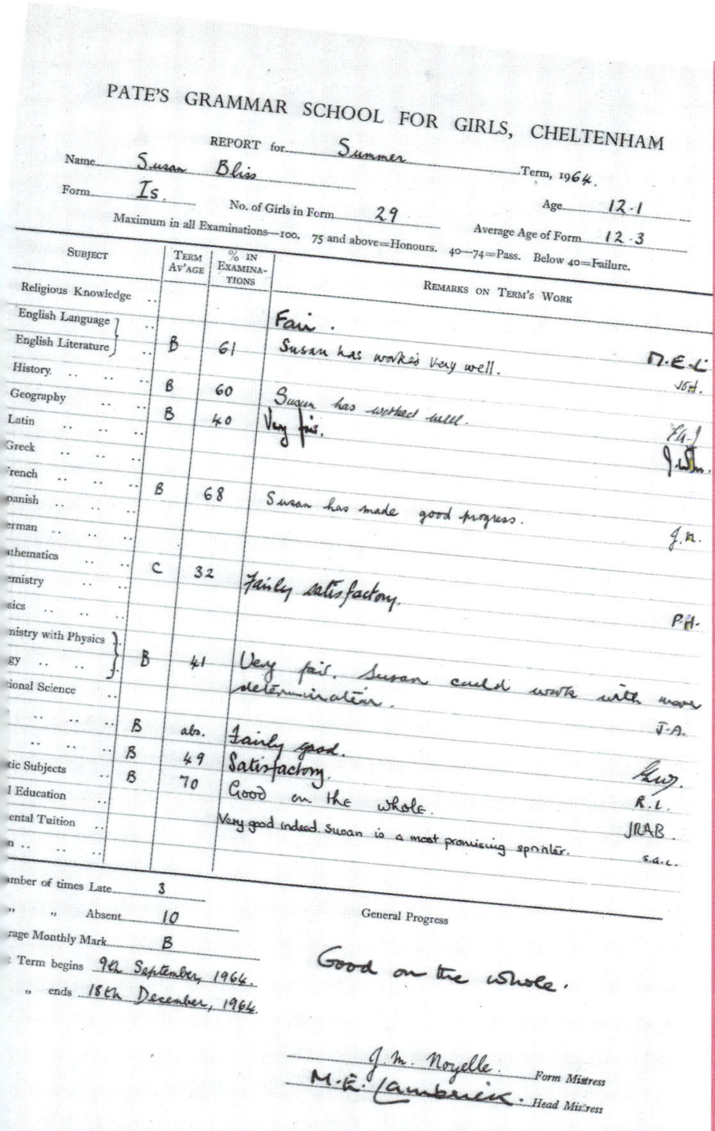

PATE'S GRAMMAR SCHOOL FOR GIRLS, CHELTENHAM

REPORT for Summer Term, 1964.

Name Susan Bliss

Form Is. No. of Girls in Form 29 Age 12·1

Maximum in all Examinations—100. 75 and above=Honours. 40—74=Pass. Below 40=Failure. Average Age of Form 12·3

SUBJECT	TERM AV'AGE	% IN EXAMINATIONS	REMARKS ON TERM'S WORK	
Religious Knowledge ..				
English Language			Fair.	
English Literature ..	B	61	Susan has worked very well.	M.E.L.
History	B	60	Susan has worked well.	JGH.
Geography	B	40	Very fair.	FU-J
Latin				
Greek				J.Wh.
'rench	B	68	Susan has made good progress.	
panish				J.N.
erman				
athematics	C	32	Fairly satisfactory.	
emistry				
sics				P.H.
nistry with Physics				
gy	B	41	Very fair. Susan could work with more determination.	
ional Science ..				
.. .. ..	B	abs.	Fairly good.	J.A.
.. .. ..	B	49	Satisfactory.	
tic Subjects ..	B	70	Good on the whole.	
l Education ..				R.L.
ental Tuition ..			Very good indeed. Susan is a most promising sprinter.	JRAB.
n				S.A.C.

umber of times Late 3

" " Absent 10

rage Monthly Mark B

: Term begins 9th September, 1964.

" ends 18th December, 1964.

General Progress

Good on the whole.

J. M. Noyelle. Form Mistress

M. E. Lambrick. Head Mistress

We were on a quiz show called "Top of the Form". It was televised from our school, I was in the audience. I was too young to answer any of the questions but it was jolly exciting to have it all going on. One of the girls from our team is an actress on TV now. The funny thing is she looks much younger now than she did then. Everyone always wanted to look older than they were.

We always tried to get away with wearing a tiny bit of make-up at school. On the bus in the morning it was a great chance to impress the sixth-form boys from the grammar school. You made sure they saw your false eyelashes before you had to whip them off just outside school. The bus conductress was really fierce. She'd stop the bus and tell any of the boys to get off if they were mucking about. There was no smoking at the back of the bus if she was on duty.

Girl Guides

I was into being a proper Girl Guide. I had every single badge you could get, except beekeeping. Dad was very proud of me. I became a Queen's Guide. That was the most you could do after you'd got all the badges.

In 1966 I went to the opening of the Severn Road Bridge. They invited the Queen's Guides to the ceremony. Our names went into a hat and mine was chosen. We were in a group from Cheltenham and we got to stand on the bridge in our uniforms.

I was very proud of my badges. My sister wasn't keen at all and only had one badge.

WESTERN DAILY PRESS BRIDGE SPECIAL, Friday,

TO WALES by NEW BUS SERVICES VIA SEVERN BRIDGE

Now it's everyone's bridge

Queen meets the Brothers Darling (both of them are generals)

The Queen met two Generals Darling yesterday.

They were brothers.

In the top picture, the Queen shares a joke at Newhouse with Major-General D. L. Darling (right), officer commanding the 53rd Welsh Division TA.

Goc-in-C

In the lower picture, on the Aust side of the bridge, Lieutenant-General Sir Kenneth Darling GOC-in-C Southern Command (right) walks behind the Queen as she prepares to inspect the guard of honour.

The Queen is escorted by Major D. H. Potter.

Even our pack leader wore a short skirt.

We went on camp, learnt to make a fire and sang songs round it in the evening. We learnt a bit of first aid which I really liked doing. I always fancied being a nurse. At home, when I was little, I had plastic dolls stuffed with kapok and I stuck pins in them to give them pretend injections. I'd have a new toy nurse's uniform every birthday, and the soft toys in our house were always ill with bandages on.

I was at the guides on the night J F Kennedy was shot. A girl who'd been told to leave the troop came rushing in with the news. I remember the pack leader was cross with her for disturbing us but we were all really stunned. People seemed shocked for days.

Da
Mi
No. 18,640
SSASSINATED
bends over her dying husband. Standing on the car bumper is a Secret Service man.
holds dying husband

THE world was horror-struck last night by the news that America's President John F. Kennedy was dead—shot down by a hidden assassin.

Mr. Kennedy, only forty-six and the leader of the West, was riding in an open car with his wife Jackie in Dallas, Texas.

A bullet ripped through his head. He fell forward, and his 34-year-old wife cradled his head in her arms.

As the car raced to a nearby hospital, Jackie kept crying: "Oh, no." Her clothes were spattered with blood.

Mr. Kennedy lived only twenty-five minutes after he was hit. In hospital, surgeons opened his throat to relieve breathing and to give him blood.

But he died—at about 1 p.m., local time, 7 p.m. British time. And shocked millions throughout the world heard the announcement soon afterwards.

Texan Governor John Connally, 46, who was in the Presidential car, was also hit by one of the assassin's three shots. After an operation his condition was satisfactory.

Waiting

Last night, police were questioning ...

Mr. Kennedy was the fourth United States President to be assassinated.

Automatically, Vice-President Johnson, 55, takes over ...

Holidays

We went camping in Wales a lot. We canoed on the river and all slept in one tent. It had two bedrooms, which was the latest thing, and was frightfully expensive. Dad had liked boats ever since he'd been in the navy. He always wrote a message home on a coconut which he threw in the sea. Sometimes they even arrived. We never went anywhere by plane but always drove or went by boat. We did go up to Heathrow sometimes just to look at the planes.

When the M50 opened we used to go and drive on it just for the treat. We'd go down to Tewkesbury and come home again. Our local MP, Gerald Nabarro, brought in the crash barriers on the motorways. The number plate on his car was Nab 1. I knew that because Dad painted his house.

We couldn't go anywhere unless there was somewhere to use our boat.

On holiday in Cornwall.

Dad's car was second-hand but it was the latest model.

When Dad got a Mark 2 Jaguar in 1964 we all went right across Europe to Yugoslavia for a holiday. It was considered a mad thing to do then. When we came home the whole family were waiting for us. They probably thought we'd never come back.

We went to London with Dad. It was quite a journey going up there by car. I was never allowed to go to London by myself. We'd go to Madame Tussauds and then go shopping. I always desperately tried to buy something in Carnaby Street. If all else failed, I'd buy a Union Jack sticker. Everything had a Union Jack on it then, even the plastic carrier bag that I used instead of a handbag. I wanted a T-shirt with a Union Jack on it but Dad wouldn't let me have one. Since he'd been in the navy he took the flag very seriously.

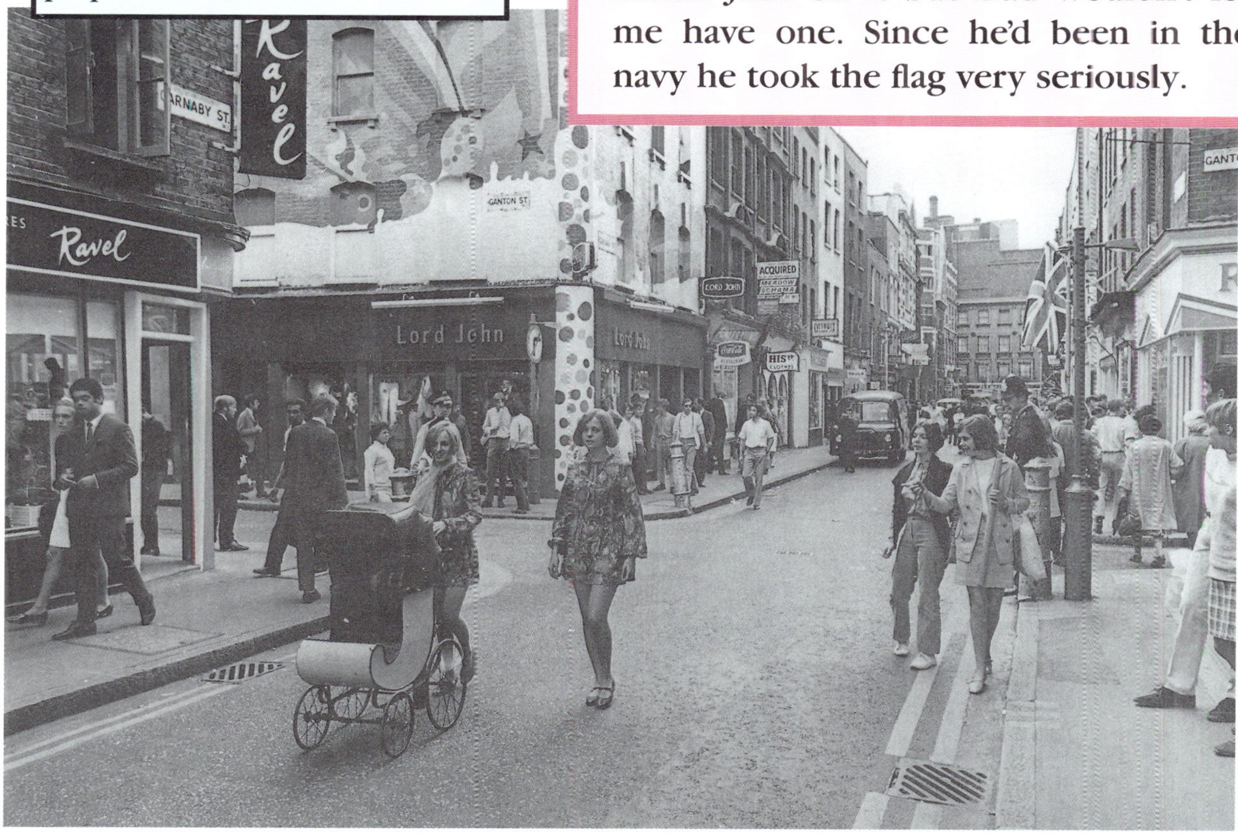

Carnaby Street, with its fashion boutiques, was popular with young people in the 1960s.

Fashions

When I was fifteen, just as soon as it was legal, I worked as a Saturday girl in the Co-op. I was on the stocking counter and earned about ten shillings a day. Later on I was moved upstairs to ladies' corsets. That was a very big department. Even girls my age had a pantie girdle then. I had a Playtex "Cross Your Heart" girdle; they were the thing to flatten your tummy. I didn't really need one since my hip bones stuck out and my tummy went in.

It was more exciting working downstairs just inside the front door because gangs of Mods and Rockers used to come in and chat up the girls on the counter. I preferred the Mods to the Rockers because I thought they looked smarter. I'd talk to them until Miss Ireland, the supervisor, got cross and sent me off for a tea-break.

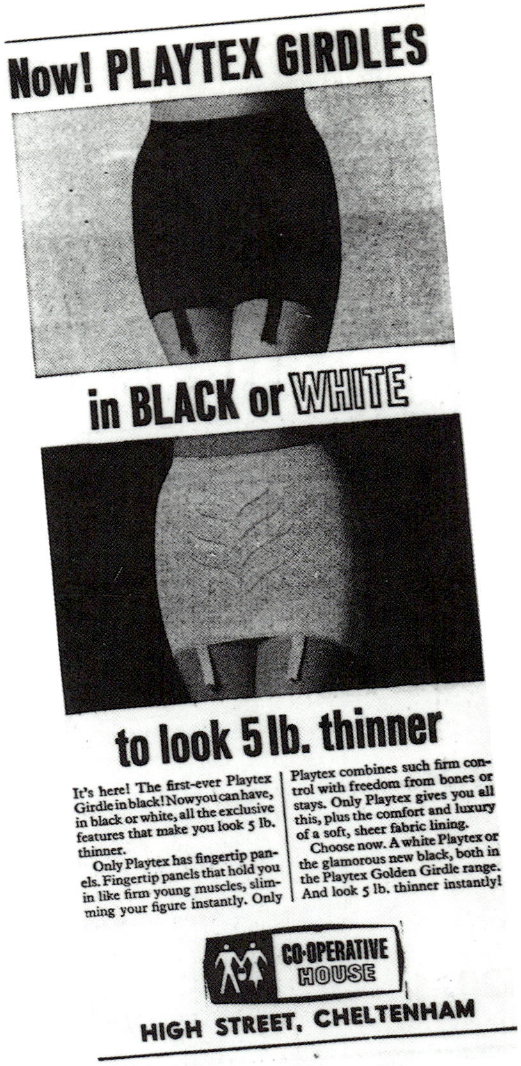

Mods wore parkas and rode scooters. They sometimes clashed with Rockers, who wore leather jackets and rode motorbikes.

I went clothes shopping with my friends Stella and Betsy. Lucy wasn't interested in fashion; she was never out of a pair of jeans. Mum bought me some clothes and I used the money from my Saturday job to buy the rest. It was very exciting when a new chain of clothes shops called Chelsea Girl came to the High Street. They sold black crêpe trousers with very wide legs, and red seersucker shirts – all my friends had that outfit.

I had green suede stiletto shoes which were really fashionable, though Dad always said they'd ruin my feet. I wore the tiniest little mini-skirt – Dad used to frown and say I'd catch cold but Mum was quite trendy so she didn't mind. After the mini came the maxi. I had a long black coat which I wore over a mini-skirt so short it was like a pelmet.

I looked just like Twiggy, or rather I thought she looked just like me.

Dresses with great big zips were all the rage. I used to hang things from the zip on mine.

It was a great thing when Biba clothes first came to Cheltenham. Everything was black or purple; black feather boas, black tights, black make-up. It all seemed amazing and terribly expensive. The ultimate was going to London to the real Biba shop. I used to go and just wander around all day and not know what to buy. Mostly I came away without anything much.

The exciting way to spend Saturday afternoon was to wander around Boots looking at the make-up. I wore thick white lipstick, matching nail varnish and heavy mascara. You could hardly lift your eyelids when you'd put it on. It took at least an hour to get ready to go out.

If we weren't window shopping, we would go to the Cadena. There were waitresses who brought you a tray of cakes to the table – you could stay there for hours. The big store called Cavendish House was wonderful for shopping. They always had someone to serve you.

Biba was the most famous of the women's fashion shops in the 1960s.

The Cadena Café is now a branch of Habitat.

Travel to India influenced the "hippy" look.

My hairpiece was made of nylon, not real hair. I went to a smart hairdresser in the Promenade during the week and left it there to be set. Then on Saturday I'd go in and have my hair done. The hairpiece was fixed on with metal pins, and then a ribbon covered the fixings. I always wore that with my mini-skirt to go to the dances at the technical college. One day in the corridor a very tall boy pushed past me and his jacket button got caught in my hairpiece. It was agony – someone had to cut us apart in the end. He lost the button off his jacket. It was dreadfully embarrassing. I was off my hairpiece for a while after that.

Boys had really long hair if they could get away with it. It was all right for students and musicians, but it was often difficult to get a job if you grew your hair too long.

Saturday night out

When I was about thirteen I was fascinated by the Youth Club in Winchcombe. It was great fun to go there and drink Coke with the boys from the secondary modern. The big thing was to have a Coke with half an aspirin dropped in. That was considered very daring. I always wanted to try it but I was a bit too scared. I knew drugs existed but they weren't a big thing at our school.

I used to walk about four kilometres home from the Youth Club along a country road at night. Hardly anyone had a car. There was only one bus in the morning and one in the afternoon, so most kids walked everywhere. Later on I was allowed to ride pillion on a boyfriend's motorbike, but I had to wear Mum's helmet.

The Youth Club that Susan went to in Winchcombe is still in use.

The Twist was a popular dance style in the 1960s.

SUNDAY MIRROR, November 8, 1964 PAGE 13

GAD, SIR! JUST LOOK WHAT'S HAPPENING IN CHELTENHAM (of all plac

CHELTENHAM has sixty schools, 150 clubs and societies, spa water, 72,000 people—and the Waikiki Wine Club, which is downstairs from the Bar B Q, a coffee bar strident with kid talk and jukey music.

The Waikiki and the Bar B Q are only a street's width from the august and genteel Queen's Hotel, heart and soul of the Cheltenham that used to be.

The old Cheltenham—smug and charming.

The Blue Moon club was above this vegetable shop in the High Street.

Later on, Dad used to pick me up by car from parties in Cheltenham. It was the thing to have parties where everyone came dressed in pyjamas. It was always utterly dark; I don't remember there being a party with a light on. No one ever knew how long you'd taken to get ready since they couldn't even see all the make-up you were wearing. Some kids had all-night parties at weekends and even managed to persuade their parents to go out for the night. Unfortunately I was always collected and taken home. Sometimes I didn't go because it was worse to be collected early than not go at all.

Sometimes we went to the clubs and coffee bars in Cheltenham. There was one club where you had to be sixteen to get in. I used to pretend to be old enough and I mostly got away with it. I was banned by my parents from a club called the Blue Moon. I don't think it was really that exciting inside but being banned made me badly want to get in.

Me and Steve, who was to become my first husband, and my cousin who played in a band.

Television and radio

We first got a television after Debbie was born. I think it was a treat for my mum. Before that we listened to the radio. I remember seeing the first ever "Coronation Street" on telly. My favourite programme was "Juke Box Jury" with David Jacobs – we had to watch that every week. There was another pop programme on ITV called "Thank Your Lucky Stars". A girl on that programme always said "I'll give it five" – that was her catch phrase. She was called Janice and had a terrific beehive hairdo. I longed for my hair to be like hers.

Everybody watched Churchill's funeral on TV. We had the day off school out of respect. When the Aberfan disaster happened I thought it looked just like my village school. It was horrible.

1

5.40
JUKE BOX JURY
A new disc—a Hit or a Miss?
Comments and opinions on the latest pop releases
This week's panel:
Joe Brown
Terence Edmond
Jackie de Shannon
and another guest
In the chair,
David Jacobs
Programme devised by
Potter
Neville Wortman

"It's definitely a hit," say the junior jury when the main jury's opinion is split over the last record

The full horror of the Aberfan disaster was brought home by the TV. A slag heap collapsed on the village school of Aberfan, killing two hundred children.

Transistor radios were new, and Grandpa bought me one for passing the "eleven plus". It was in a tan leather case, and there was a little flap with a button over the batteries. I was really proud of it. I listened to Radio Luxemburg every evening as soon as it came on; it was terribly crackly. Later on I listened to Radio Caroline, the pirate station, that was on all day. My favourite songs then were "If you're going to San Francisco" and "A Whiter Shade of Pale".

Everyone I knew had a go at playing the guitar, mostly badly. There were lots of Cheltenham bands. We thought they were more famous than the Beatles. They drove around in old vans with their names on the side. I used to hang around hoping someone famous would step out, but they never did.

Radio Caroline broadcasted from a ship off-shore because the government wouldn't give them a licence.

Music

At school we had a great crush on the Beatles. Each gang of girls shared them out. I had Ringo and I thought he was the best because he was going to be mine. He was the ugly one so there wasn't as much competition as for the others. I had posters of him all over the walls of my bedroom.

I bought each of the Beatles' singles as soon as they came out. Dad had an account at the local DIY shop and the chap there discovered he could make extra money selling us singles and putting them down as paint. Dad found out, of course, and put a stop to it.

My Auntie Ethel took me to see the Beatles film, "Magical Mystery Tour". She thought they were wonderful, "So clean and wholesome" she said.

The Beatles caused so much excitement amongst their fans that the newspapers described it as "Beatlemania".

I was at school with Brian Jones' sister. He was the lead guitarist with the Rolling Stones and sometimes he came back to Cheltenham. Dad said I mustn't have anything to do with him but he needn't have worried. I thought the Stones were ghastly, they were a scruffy lot. The only record of theirs I bought was "Paint it Black".

There weren't many concerts in Gloucestershire; the best we had was Billy J Kramer live at the Odeon. It was a great big place then and you couldn't hear a thing at the back with everybody screaming. Gene Pitney appeared quite often. I got through the side gate once to the stage door and waited for him to come out. Of course when he did I didn't know what to say.

The Rolling Stones gave a free concert in London's Hyde Park after the death of Brian Jones. Mick Jagger read a poem in his memory.

ODEON CINEMA, Winchcombe Street (Tel. 24081)

Sunday, January 30th for Seven Days
"HEROES OF TELEMARK" (U), with Kirk Douglas and Richard Harris.

Sunday, February 6th for Seven Days
Please see Press and Theatre Announcements.

Sunday, February 13th for Six Days (Saturday Excepted)
"THE HALLELUJAH TRAIL" (A). Burt Lancaster, Lee Remick, Jim Hutton, Pamela Tiffin, Donald Pleasence, Brian Keith, Martin Landau.

Saturday, February 19th for One Day Only
On the Stage. GENE PITNEY, Len Barry, The Mike Cotton Sound, The Just 5, Billy Boyle, Sue and Sunny, Dave, Dee, Dozy, Beaky, Mick and Tich. Two performances: 6.15 and 8.45. Seats 12/6, 10/6, 9/6, 8/6.

Sunday, February 20th for Seven Days
Walt Disney's "THAT DARN CAT!" (U). Hayley Mills, Dean Jones, Dorothy Provine, Roddy McDowall, Neville Brand, Ed Wynn.
"GERONIMO'S REVENGE" (U). Tom Tryon, Darryl Hickman, Betty Lynn.

Sunday, February 27th for Seven Days
Ian Fleming's "THUNDERBALL" (A). Sean Connery, Claudine Auger, Adolfo Celi, Luciana Paluzzi, Rik Van Nutter.

The Odeon is now a five-screen cinema.

Leaving school

You could either be a nurse or a teacher when you left our school. When one girl went off to become an engineer it was announced at assembly and we all felt very proud of her. I'd always wanted to be a nurse so it wasn't a problem deciding what to do after school.

I did ten O-levels and passed all of them except Latin. I left school and did a pre-nursing course while I waited till I was eighteen and could start as a full-time student nurse. I got paid £28 a month to begin with. I worked in hospitals for several years and then became the nursing sister in a boarding school.

Now I run a consultancy firm in Cheltenham, helping charities to raise money.

I am the third nurse from the right.

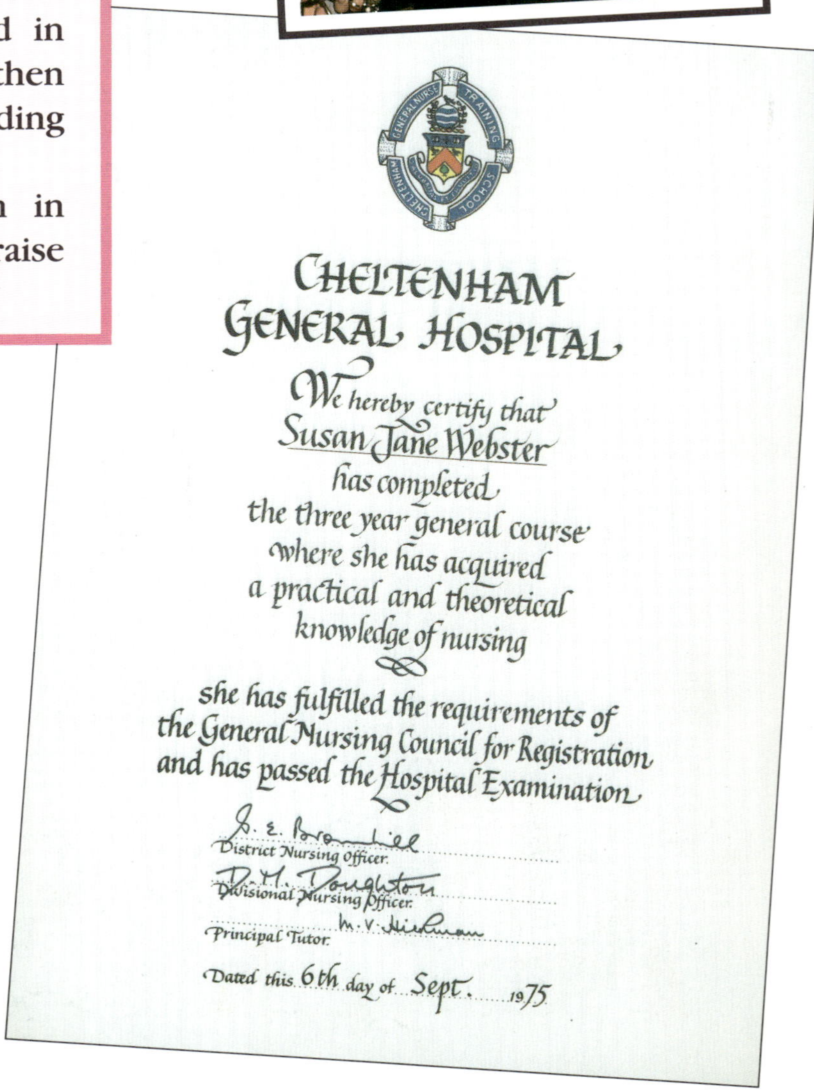

CHELTENHAM GENERAL HOSPITAL

We hereby certify that Susan Jane Webster has completed the three year general course where she has acquired a practical and theoretical knowledge of nursing

she has fulfilled the requirements of the General Nursing Council for Registration and has passed the Hospital Examination

District Nursing Officer.

Divisional Nursing Officer.

Principal Tutor.

Dated this 6th day of Sept. 1975

In the news

These are some of the important events which happened during Susan's childhood.

1960 In the black township of Sharpeville, the South African police shot and killed fifty-six protesters against the government.

1961 In Germany the Berlin Wall was completed by the Communists to prevent East Germans travelling to the West.

1962 Nelson Mandela, the forty-four-year-old black South African leader, was imprisoned.

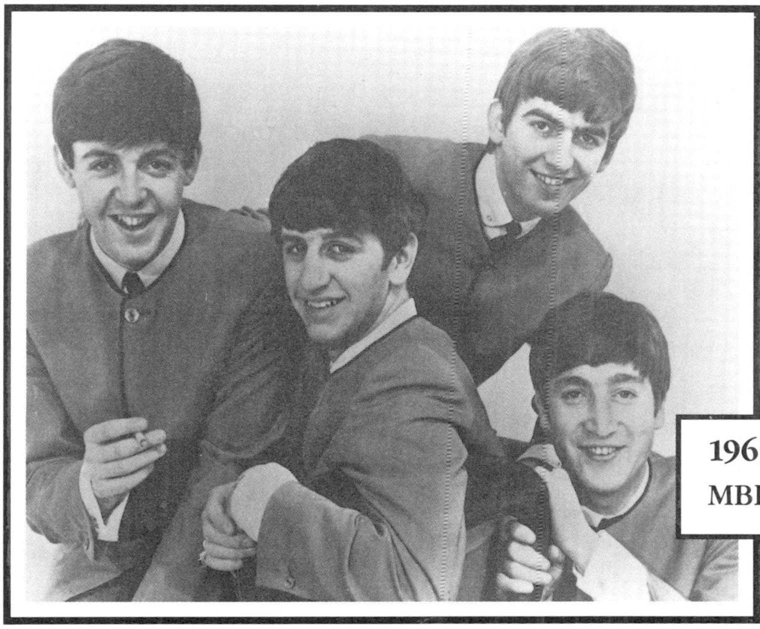

1965 The Beatles each received the MBE from the Queen.

1966 England won the World Cup at Wembley with Bobby Moore as captain.

1967 In China the Red Guards forced the people to follow the thoughts of Chairman Mao Tse-Tung. Individuals were publicly punished for disobeying.

1968 There was a large demonstration outside the American Embassy, in London's Grosvenor Square, against American involvement in Vietnam.

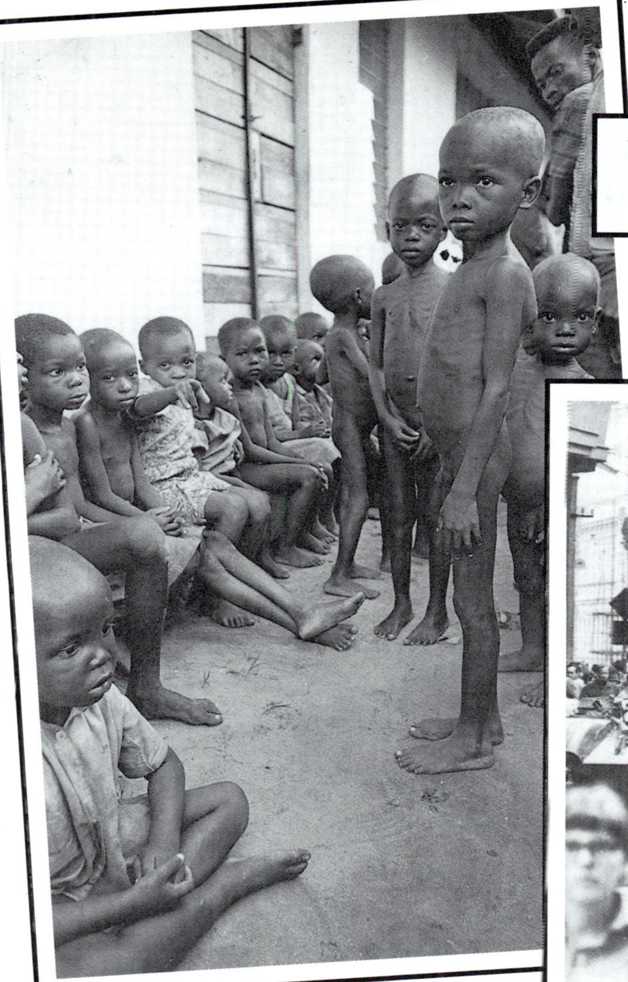

1968 Civil war in Nigeria caused mass starvation in the state of Biafra.

1968 The Soviet government sent in troops to prevent reforms in Czechoslovakia.

1969 American astronauts made the first manned landing on the Moon.

Things to do

Make a 1960's scrapbook

Many of your relatives or neighbours will have memories of the 1960s. Their experiences may have been very different from those of Susan Forbes. Show them this book and ask them how their life in the 1960s compared.

If you have a cassette recorder you could tape their memories. Before you visit people, make a list of the things you want to talk about – for example, music, clothes, films, school, sports. Some people may have kept photos of the period as well as magazines or records. Ask if you can look at them.

Make a list of musicians who were popular in the 1960s. Find out how many of them are still making records now. Look at fashion from the 1960s, then see if you can find similar styles in today's magazines.

Go to your local library. Look at books about homes and entertainment. Compare how things looked in the 1960s with how they look now. Your library may have a local studies section. If so, ask to see photographs of your area from the 1960s. Compare places then with what is there today.

Look at the front pages of some old newspapers (or at the endpapers of this book) to see if you can recognise any people from the news on TV today.

Use what you find out to make a scrapbook about the 1960s.

Reading list: here is a list of other books to read on the 1960s.

Decades: The Sixties
Tim Healey (Wayland)

Finding out about life in Britain in the 1960s
Nigel Richardson (Batsford)

Growing up in the 1960s
Richard Tames (Batsford)

History of the Modern World: The Sixties
Nathaniel Harris (Macdonald Educational)

Picture History of the Twentieth Century
Tim Healey (Franklin Watts)

Portrait of a Decade: The 1960s
Trevor Fisher (Batsford)

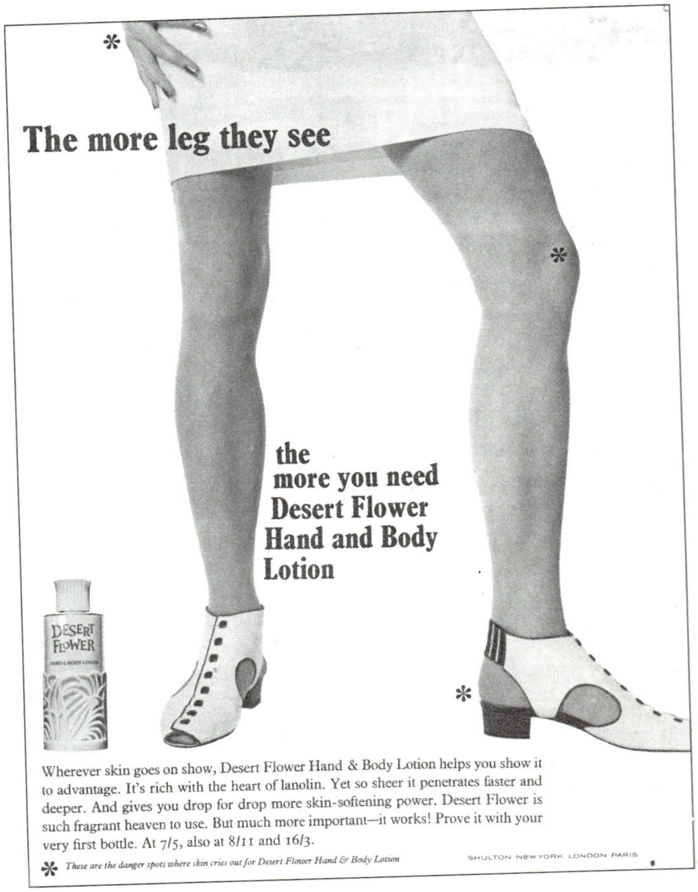

Page 2—MELODY MAKER, November 15, 1969

Melody Maker POP 30

1 (1) SUGAR SUGAR .... Archies, RCA
2 (2) OH WELL .... Fleetwood Mac, Reprise
3 (5) RETURN OF DJANGO .... Upsetters, Upsetter
4 (3) HE AIN'T HEAVY . . . HE'S MY BROTHER ... Hollies, Parlophone
5 (4) I'M GONNA MAKE YOU MINE .... Lou Christie, Buddah
6 (12) WONDERFUL WORLD, BEAUTIFUL PEOPLE Jimmy Cliff, Trojan
7 (7) DELTA LADY .... Joe Cocker, Regal Zonophone
8 (11) LOVE'S BEEN GOOD TO ME .... Frank Sinatra, Reprise
9 (25) (CALL ME) NUMBER ONE .... Tremeloes, CBS
10 (9) NOBODY'S CHILD .... Karen Young, Major Minor
11 (6) SPACE ODDITY .... David Bowie, Philips
12 (26) SOMETHING .... Beatles, Apple
13 (16) WHAT DOES IT TAKE
Jnr. Walker and the All Stars, Tamla Motown
14 (10) A BOY NAMED SUE .... Johnny Cash, CBS
15 (8) I'LL NEVER FALL IN LOVE AGAIN ..... Bobbie Gentry, Capitol
16 (15) DO WHAT YOU GOTTA DO .... Four Tops, Tamla Motown
17 (23) SWEET DREAM .... Jethro Tull, Chrysalis
18 (18) LONG SHOT (KICK THE BUCKET) .... Pioneers, Trojan
19 (27) COLD TURKEY .... Plastic Ono Band, Apple
20 (22) LIQUIDATOR .... Harry J and the All Stars, Trojan
21 (13) LAY LADY LAY .... Bob Dylan, CBS
22 (14) JE T'AIME MOI NON PLUS
Jane Birkin and Serge Gainsbourg, Major Minor
23 (17) EVERYBODY'S TALKING .... Nilsson, RCA
24 (—) RUBY DON'T TAKE YOUR LOVE TO TOWN
Kenny Rogers and the 1st Edition, Reprise
25 (24) AND THE SUN WILL SHINE .... Jose Feliciano, RCA
26 (19) IT'S GETTING BETTER .... Mama Cass, Stateside
27 (—) NO MULE'S FOOL .... Family, Reprise
28 (20) BAD MOON RISING ..... Creedence Clearwater Revival, Liberty
29 (—) BILJO .... Clodagh Rodgers, RCA
30 (21) GOOD MORNING STARSHINE .... Oliver, CBS

POP 30 PUBLISHERS

1 Welbeck; 2 Fleetwood Music; 3 Island/B & C; 4 Cyril Shane; 5 Carlin; 6 Island; 7 Alan Keen Music; 8 Ambassador; 9 Gale; 10 Acuff-Rose; 11 Essex; 12 Harrisongs; 13 Jobete Carlin; 14 Copyright Control; 15 Blue Sea/Jac; 16 Carlin; 17 Chrysalis; 18 Blue Mountain; 19 Northern Songs; 20 Island/B & C; 21 Feldman; 22 Shapiro Bernstein; 23 April; 24 Southern; 25 Abigail; 26 Screen Gems; 27 Copyright Control; 28 Burlington; 29 Kangaroo April; 30 United Artists

top twenty albums

1 (1) **ABBEY ROAD** Beatles .... Apple
2 (2) **JOHNNY CASH AT SAN QUENTIN** Johnny Cash .... CBS
3 (3) **TAMLA MOTOWN CHARTBUSTERS Vol 3** Various Artists ... Tamla Motown
4 (11) **IN THE COURT OF THE CRIMSON KING** King Crimson .... Island
5 (4) **THROUGH THE PAST DARKLY** Rolling Stones .... Decca
6 (14) **LED ZEPPELIN II** Led Zeppelin .... Atlantic
7 (7) **THEN PLAY ON** Fleetwood Mac Reprise
8 (5) **SSSSH** Ten Years After ...... Deram
9 (6) **HAIR** London Cast .... Polydor
18 (8) **BLIND FAITH** Blind Faith ... Polydor
11 (16) **STAND UP** Jethro Tull .... Island
12 (9) **OLIVER** Soundtrack .... RCA
13 (17) **THE BEST OF CREAM** Cream Polydor
14 (10) **SONGS FOR A TAILOR** Jack Bruce ... Polydor
15 (12) **NASHVILLE SKYLINE** Bob Dylan CBS
(15) **THE WORLD OF MANTOVANI Vol 2** Mantovani .... Decca
17 (—) **UMMAGUMMA** Pink Floyd ...... Harvest
18 (—) **A MAN ALONE** Frank Sinatra Reprise
19 (—) **NICE ENOUGH TO EAT** Various Artists Island
20 (—) **THE BEST OF THE BEE GEES** Bee Gees Polydor

Two titles tied for 15th position.

u.s. top ten

As listed by "Billboard"

1 (1) **WEDDING BELL BLUES** Fifth Dimension .... Soul City
2 (8) **COME TOGETHER** Beatles ...... Apple
3 (2) **SOMETHING** Beatles .... Apple
4 (3) **SUSPICIOUS MINDS** Elvis Presley RCA
5 (4) **BABY IT'S YOU** Smith ...... Dunhill
6 (9) **AND WHEN I DIE** Blood, Sweat and Tears .... Columbia
7 (7) **SMILE A LITTLE SMILE FOR ME** Flying Machine .... Congress
8 (5) **TRACY** Cuff Links .... Decca
9 (—) **TAKE A LETTER MARIA** R. B. Greaves Atco
10 (6) **SUGAR SUGAR** Archies ..... Calendar

Index

Series design: David Bennett
Design: Mel Raymond
Editor: Jenny Wood

Picture research: Sarah Ridley

Acknowledgements: thanks to Helen Bliss Williams, Mr H Rhodes and to Susan Forbes, without whom this book would not have been possible.

Photography: Neil Thomson.

Additional photographs: thanks to Apple/EMI 24c; Camera Press 25t; Cheltenham Art Gallery and Museum 18b, 21c; thanks to Ford Motor Company Archives 31br; John Frost Newspaper Service 12br, 13br, 17br, 23t; thanks to the Girl Guide Association 13bl; International Defence and Aid Fund for South Africa 27cr; thanks to Mrs R Lane 5b; thanks to Sue Limb 9br; Robert Opie 22t; Popperfoto cover tl, cover tr, 16b, 22b, 24b, 27t, 27cl, 27b, 28t, 28c, 29(all); Penzance Town Council 14b; thanks to Mr Rhodes, Gretton Primary School 8c; Telecom Technology Showcase 7t; Topham Picture Library 15b, 17t, 19b, 20b, 23b, 28b; Vintage Magazine Company 24t, 31l, 31tr.

The publishers have endeavoured to discover the copyright holders of material reproduced in this book. However, if anyone can give any further information, please let us know.

A CIP Catalogue record for this book is available from the British Library.

Printed in Belgium.

PRINTED IN BELGIUM BY proost INTERNATIONAL BOOK PRODUCTION

THE DAILY TELEGRAPH AND MORNING POST, FRIDAY, FEBRUARY 2, 1968.

COLOUR MAGAZINE TODAY

The Daily Telegraph

No. 35075. LONDON, FRIDAY, FEBRUARY 2, 1968. and Morning Post Printed in LONDON and MANCHESTER. 4d.

6,200 Viet Cong killed

'ALL OR NOTHING' BATTLE FOR SAIGON

Bombing continues, says Johnson

WORST 'YET TO COME'

TWELVE THOUSAND North Vietnamese and Viet Cong troops have been sent to Saigon and its surrounding provinces alone in the Communists' ferocious "all or nothing" battle to gain control of South Vietnam's capital and provincial cities.

As a result President Johnson said in Washington last night that American bombing of North Vietnam would continue. American Servicemen in Vietnam would "not fail us, even if it means dying before another morning comes."

As the battle for the cities enters its fourth day today, the latest casualty figures are:

COMMUNISTS: 6,200 dead, 2,500 captured.

ALLIES: 550 dead (193 American), 1,898 wounded (929 American).

Totals are expected to be far higher when full figures have been collected.

Gen. Westmoreland, American commander in Vietnam, said yesterday that the worst of the fighting was still to come. An enemy attempt to conquer South Vietnam's two northernmost provinces, where 50,000 Communist troops have massed, including 20,000 around America's Khe Sanh base, was expected "any time."

The general said Hanoi had approved its "all or nothing" campaign to crush the allies last September. The first phase, enlarging bases and psychological, lasted until mid-January. The second was the battle of the cities, and the third would be the northern all-out assault.

HQ IN CHINATOWN PAGODA

Savage street fighting was continuing in darkness in Saigon last night after a day in which South Vietnamese planes three times bombed evacuated suburbs where Communists are holding out.

Just before dusk South Vietnamese troops broke into the An Quang pagoda in Cholon, the capital's Chinatown, where the Viet Cong had had their headquarters and had established a "revolutionary council" to run the city.

The Communists were said to have been split into small groups by last night, but on the south side of the city Americans with tanks were involved in "extremely heavy" fighting with "neither side giving an inch."

At least 2,000 civilians are believed to have been killed or wounded in Saigon, where a 24-hour curfew as well as martial law has been imposed. The South Vietnamese Government last night introduced censorship.

COMMUNISTS HOLD HUE

There was fighting in almost all important provincial towns. In the north, Americans gained control of most of the city of Quang Tri, but were repulsed when they tried to dislodge Communists controlling the centre of the ancient capital of Hue, where a second "revolutionary government" was established.

American infantry was sent to the mountain resort town of Dalat, 140 miles north-east of Saigon, which was overrun by Communists yesterday.

About a thousand Viet Cong were in control of the Central Highlands town of Kontrum and continuous small-arms fire forced the American air base there to close. America's biggest airbase in Vietnam at Bien Hoa, near Saigon, was attacked last night and unconfirmed reports said large fires could be seen.

The North Vietnamese Government, which warned the people of Hanoi to prepare for retaliatory bombing raids, claimed yesterday that the Viet Cong were in a position to win a complete victory.

Russia admitted publicly for the first time that she is supplying arms to the Viet Cong. Mr. Kosygin, Prime Minister, said in Kabul, capital of Afghanistan, that it was "an open secret that our weapons are used by the patriots."

TALKS WITH N. KOREA

On the second Far East crisis front, Korea, the United States yesterday accepted a North Korean suggestion that the capture of the intelligence ship Pueblo should be discussed through the Military Armistice Commission at Panmunjon.

A third American aircraft carrier, the Ranger, 60,000 tons, has joined the American fleet off North Korea.

Revenge in battle-torn street

GENERAL Nguyen Ngoc Loan, chief of South Vietnam's national police, shooting a Viet Cong officer in civilian disguise in Saigon yesterday. He said later: "They killed many Americans and many of my people." LOWER: A South Vietnamese officer carrying his dead child from his home where he found his family killed by the Viet Cong. Other pictures—P20.

Viet Cong set up 'government'

FROM OUR CORRESPONDENT
TOKYO, Thursday.

HANOI radio claimed tonight that the Viet Cong offensives in Saigon and Hue had been so successful that revolutionary governments had been established in both cities.

The rebel government, known as the "Alliance of National, Democratic and Peace Forces," had issued an urgent manifesto demanding that America and its allies withdraw all troops from South Vietnam to end the war.

It had called for negotiations with the "South Vietnam National Liberation Front on measures to restore peace and regain national independence and sovereignty."

The radio monitored in Tokyo, went on: "The alliance's manifesto has been welcomed by many prominent personalities, intellectuals, industrialists, businessmen and religious people in Saigon."

Bitter Fighting and U.S. Drops Bombing Pause—Back Page
Westmoreland's Warning, Washington Gloom, Pueblo Talks Concession, and Cartoon—P21
Pictures—P20
Editorial Comment—P16

Hanoi Radio and the Viet Cong radio later joined in announcing formation of provincial governments in Quang Tri, Thua Thien and Hue.

"President" named

Both stations quoted reports from a North Vietnamese correspondent in Saigon naming the new Saigon Government's president as Le Van Hao, doctor of ethnology and professor of Saigon and Hue universities.

In an appeal read over the Hue radio tonight, Professor Hao is purported to have said: "We cannot stand with folded arms and see our country fall into the hands of the United States aggressors and the Thieu-Ky clique of traitors. We can no longer endure the life of slavery, exploitation, poverty and misery."

The radio stations called on South Vietnamese troops and police to turn their guns on their officers and the Americans and to raise the black, red, and gold Viet Cong flag as a sign of Viet Cong victory.

NIGHT OF RETRIBUTION, SAYS MOSCOW

Referring to the fighting in Vietnam, Moscow Radio said last night: "The night of retribution is now on." The "liberation forces know that they have the support of the Soviet Union."

Russia had given and would continue to give "all round help until the invasion troops get out of Vietnam."

Peking Radio applauded the Viet Cong for their "most inspiring victories."

Index to Other Pages

Jones challenged on bus pay by Cousins

By ROBERT BEDLOW
Industrial Staff

MR. FRANK COUSINS, general secretary of the Transport and General Workers' Union, challenged Mr. Aubrey Jones, chairman of the Prices and Incomes Board, yesterday to hold its inquiry into the "frozer" £1-a-week pay rise for 77,000 municipal busmen in public.

At the same time, he expressed doubts about the board's ability to produce an unbiased report.

In a letter to Mr. Jones, the transport workers' chief said: "We feel very strongly that any hearing of this case by your board should take place at the earliest possible moment and in public. We make this as a firm request."

Six-month delay

Last week the Government made a direction under Part II of the Prices and Incomes Act forbidding employers to pay the agreed rise and effectively blocked it for six months by referring it to the board for investigation. The union has since launched claims for county court hearings against employers

In his letter, Mr. Cousins makes the union's opposition to the reference clear and says it is a further indication of the Government's intention to apply a rigid system of wages control.

Mr. Cousins said: "There is also some anxiety as to whether your board is able to give an unbiased judgment on the issue having regard to the comments previously made on the municipal busmen's wage claim." Mr. Jones was considering Mr. Cousins's request for a public hearing last night

Industrial News—P24

£1m LOST BY ATOM PLANT BREAKDOWN

A breakdown at one of the four reactors at the Chapelcross nuclear power station at Annan, Dumfriesshire, will cost at least £1 million in lost power sales, the Atomic Energy Authority said yesterday.

A spokesman said repairs on the faulty No 2 reactor, which has been shut down since last May are likely to take several more months.

£25,000 BOND PRIZE

The winning number for the ninth £25,000 Premium Savings Bond draw is 1AF 387295. It is the first time a £1 bond bought singly, has won the prize since the draw was introduced in February, 1966. Winning numbers for £5,000, £1,000 and £500 in the 129th draw appear on Page 24.

TRAINING SCHOOL SHIP TO CLOSE

DAILY TELEGRAPH REPORTER

THE training ship Mercury on the Hamble near Southampton is to close as a secondary school after 83 years. It prepared boys for the Royal and Merchant Navies.

Cdr. Ronald Hoyle, the captain, said last night that falling numbers and rising costs were responsible. There are 120 pupils and a staff of 10. Fees are £315 a year.

The school was started in 1885 by Charles Hoare, and run by C. B. Fry, the cricketer, and his wife Beatrice, from 1908 until 1950.

ROSE GETS OVATION

BLUFF, New Zealand, Thursday.

Lone British yachtsman, Mr. Alec Rose, 59, in his yacht, Lively Lady, was towed into this southernmost New Zealand port tonight for rigging repairs. He received a hero's welcome from hundreds of people.

LATE NEWS

POLICE RAIDS

By Our Crime Correspondent

Detectives recovered stolen property valued at several thousand pounds in series of raids in West London last night. Two men arrested.

FOREST FIRES

Santiago, Chile, Thursday.—Chilean Government today mobilised military and agriculture Ministry resources to fight 50 forest fires in forest belt south of Santiago.

6

Personal Column—Page 18

Labour 'rebel' No. 2 chooses suspension

BY OUR POLITICAL STAFF

ANOTHER Left-Wing Labour M.P., Mr. George Perry (Nottingham S.), has written to Mr. John Silkin, Government Chief Whip, accepting voluntarily the one month's suspension from party privileges inflicted on 24 "rebels" on Wednesday.

Mr. Perry, who has frequently abstained, was absent ill during the confidence vote in Jan. 18. Mr. Ian Mikardo, who was abroad, has already volunteered to share the "punishment." Mr. Perry wrote:

In the event, I found myself unwittingly paired with a member of the opposition and therefore escaped the suspension meted out to my 24 colleagues.

This leaves me in an untenable position and, accordingly, I do not intend to avail myself to the full privileges of the Parliamentary Labour Party between now and Feb. 28.

'REBELS'' AMENDMENTS

Code of conduct

A liaison committee's proposals which would allow the "rebels" to vote on the code of conduct on their return to party privileges after Feb. 28 ran into trouble at last night's meeting of the Parliamentary party.

Mr. Douglas Houghton, chairman, disclosed that he had received amendments to the draft code from some of the "rebels."

Continued on Back Page, Col. 5

ROBINSON REJECTS CALL TO RESIGN

Mr. Robinson has told his constituency Labour party, St. Pancras North, that he will not resign as Minister of Health in protest against prescription charges. The local management committee of the party asked him to resign after discussing the charges with him last Tuesday week

In a letter he has sent to the party Mr. Robinson said he had nothing to add to what he has already told members.

HUNTING PACKS OUT AGAIN

Fox hunting was yesterday resumed outside the areas infected by the foot-and-mouth epidemic, the first time many packs had been out this season.

Hunting can now be resumed in 23 counties. They are: Cornwall, Devon, Somerset, Dorset, Wilts, Hampshire, the Isle of Wight, Berkshire, Surrey, Sussex, Kent, Pembroke, Cardigan, Carmarthen, Glamorgan, Northumberland, Durham, Cumberland, Westmorland, North Riding of Yorkshire, Anglesey, Brecon and Monmouth.

There was one fresh outbreak of foot-and-mouth disease in the 24 hours to 5 p.m. yesterday.

Tories Attack Peart—Back Page

Today's Weather

GENERAL SITUATION: Unstable W airstream covers Britain. Weak troughs of low pressure expected to cross most areas.

LONDON, E. ANGLIA, CEN. S., E. ENGLAND, MIDLANDS: Mainly dry, good sunny periods. Slight to moderate frost early and late. Winds W., light or moderate. Rather cold. Max. 41F (5C).

CHANNEL IS., S.W. ENGLAND, S. WALES: Scattered showers, good sunny periods. Wind W., moderate. Rather cold. 43F (6C).

N. WALES, N.W. ENGLAND, CEN. N. ENGLAND, LAKE DIST., S.W. SCOTLAND, GLASGOW AREA N. IRELAND: Variable cloud wintry showers, heavy at times, hail and thunder. Winds W., moderate or strong. 39F (4C).

ENGLISH CHANNEL: Moderate. IRISH SEA: Rough or very rough.

OUTLOOK: Rather cold, unsettled.

Weather Maps, Reports—P14

COST OF STANDARD LOAF UP $1\frac{1}{2}$d

INCREASE NOT ENOUGH, SAYS BAKERY GROUP

By ROLAND GRIBBEN
Business Correspondent

BREAD price increases of $1\frac{1}{2}$d on the standard loaf and 1d for a small loaf were authorised yesterday by Mr. Peart, Minister of Agriculture. [Commons Statement—P25]

Reaction from bakery groups, which had sought a 2d increase to cover rising costs and dearer wheat, was mixed. One of the four market leaders, Rank, Hovis McDougall, expressed disappointment and said that the increase should have been larger because of the accumulated costs being carried by the industry.

The increases, the eighth in as many years, are expected to add £26 million to Britain's annual bread bill of £320 million.

The Ministry of Agriculture estimates that they will increase the bread outlay for a family of three by about $7\frac{1}{2}$d a week. The rises push the recommended retail price of the standard $1\frac{3}{4}$lb loaf up to 1s $5\frac{1}{2}$d, unwrapped, and 1s $6\frac{1}{2}$d for the sliced and wrapped products.

The basic price of the small, unwrapped loaf will be $10\frac{1}{2}$d, and 1d more for the wrapped brands.

THREE HEADINGS

Wheat prices up

Mr. Peart indicated in a written Commons answer yesterday that the increase was under three headings.

The first was $\frac{1}{2}$d to cover post-devaluation rises in wheat prices; the second, $\frac{1}{2}$d to improve the rate of return on new investment as recommended by the Prices and Incomes Board a year ago; and the third, $\frac{1}{2}$d for other increased production costs, notably wages, fuel and distribution.

About 80 per cent. of wheat used in bread-making is imported, and the groups sought increases of between 8s to 11s 6d a sack for bakers' flour, used largely in England and Wales, and 12s to 15s a sack for Springs' flour, Scotland's main flour which is almost exclusively imported.

FLOUR PEGGED

Peart's warning

But the Prices Board pegged the increases at 8s 3d a sack for bakers' flour and 12s 1d for Springs' flour, and because of the stocks position, pointed out that the effects of devaluation would not be felt until mid-February.

Accordingly, Mr. Peart has deferred the bread price increases until Feb. 12.

He warned yesterday that the bread and flour increases were the "maximum justifiable," and indicated that the Government would step in to prevent any higher increases.

City Comment—P2
Commons Statement—P25
Editorial Comment—P16

PRINCESS MARGARET OPERATION

DAILY TELEGRAPH REPORTER

PRINCESS MARGARET went into the King Edward VII's Hospital for Officers, Marylebone, last night to have her tonsils removed.

The operation is expected to take place today. The Princess, who is 37, is expected to be in hospital for about a week.

She is being attended by Mr. Cecil Hogg, 67, aurist to the Queen, and Sir Ronald Bodley Scott, 62, the Queen's physician.

Princess Margaret was driven to the hospital from Kensington Palace by her husband, the Earl of Snowdon. She arrived shortly after 10 p.m.

The British Medical Association said last night that the operation, though by no means unusual, was "a bit more of an operation" with adults.

Post-operative "throat"

OUR MEDICAL CONSULTANT writes: Tonsillectomy in a patient of 37 is usually performed for chronically infected tonsils, sometimes with glandular enlargement in the neck. The patient has a sore throat post-operatively for two or three days.

PASSPORTS FOR 10 YEARS

Passports are to be issued for one period of 10 years from Monday instead of two periods of five years. Mr. Goronwy Roberts, Minister of State, Foreign Office, announced in a written Commons reply yesterday.

Children under 16 will still have passports issued for five years in the first instance, renewable for a further five years without fee on production of new photographs and personal descriptions.

The fee for the 10-year passport will be £2, a reduction of 10s on the present total cost over the same period.